A TRUE BOOK™

The National Anthem

ELAINE LANDAU

Children's Press®
A Division of Scholastic Inc.
New York Toronto London Auckland Sydney
Mexico City New Delhi Hong Kong
Danbury, Connecticut

Content Consultant

David R. Smith, PhD

Academic Adviser and Adjunct Assistant Professor of History

University of Michigan–Ann Arbor

Reading Consultant

Linda Cornwell

Literacy Consultant

Carmel, Indiana

Library of Congress Cataloging-in-Publication Data

Landau, Elaine.
The national anthem / by Elaine Landau.
    p. cm.—(A true book)
Includes bibliographical references and index.
ISBN-13: 978-0-531-12633-2 (lib. bdg.)   978-0-531-14783-2 (pbk.)
ISBN-10: 0-531-12633-1 (lib. bdg.)   0-531-14783-5 (pbk.)
1. Star-spangled banner (Song)—Juvenile literature. 2. Baltimore,
Battle of, Baltimore, Md., 1814—Juvenile literature. 3. Key, Francis
Scott, 1779–1843—Juvenile literature. I. Title. II. Series.
ML3561.S8L35 2008
782.42'15990973—dc22   2007004486

All rights reserved. Published in 2008 by Children's Press, an imprint of Scholastic Inc. Published simultaneously in Canada. Printed in the United States of America.
SCHOLASTIC, CHILDREN'S PRESS, A TRUE BOOK, and associated logos are trademarks and/or registered trademarks of Scholastic Inc.
1 2 3 4 5 6 7 8 9 10 R 17 16 15 14 13 12 11 10 09 08

Find the Truth!

Everything you are about to read is true *except* for one of the sentences on this page.

Which one is **TRUE**?

T or F   "The Star-Spangled Banner" was written the morning after a raging battle.

T or F   The writer of "The Star-Spangled Banner" wrote the words to another country's national anthem.

Find the answer in this book.

3

Contents

THE **BIG** TRUTH!

Only one man —
Rabindranath Tagore —
wrote the words to two
countries' national anthems.

5

Performer Kelly Clarkson sings the national anthem before a football game in Irving, Texas.

Name That Tune

Only one-third of Americans know the words to the national anthem.

Can you guess what the name of this song is? It is a song about the U.S. flag and an important battle in the United States of America. People often sing it before ball games, at official ceremonies, and during Fourth of July celebrations.

Baltimore Orioles players line up for the national anthem before a home game.

Did you guess "The Star-Spangled **Banner**"? If you did, you are right. "The Star-Spangled Banner" is our **national anthem**. A national anthem is a special **patriotic** song. Many nations around the world have a national anthem. Anthems are meaningful songs. People listen to and sing them to show their pride for their country.

We usually don't sing our national anthem when we are alone. We sing it with other people. It is a way to show that we are united and proud to be Americans.

Anthems Around the World

	Canada	"O Canada"
	India	"Jana Gana Mana" ("Thou Art the Ruler of the Minds of All People")
	Japan	"Kimigayo" ("May 1,000 Years of Happy Reign Be Yours")
	Mexico	"Himno Nacional Mexicano" ("Mexican National Anthem")
	Russia	"Gosudarstvenny Gimn Rossiyskoy Federatsii" ("Hymn of the Russian Federation")
	South Africa	"Nkosi Sikelel' iAfrica" ("God Bless Africa")
	United Kingdom	"God Save the Queen"

9

The British took U.S. soldiers by force to serve in the British navy. The Americans fought back in the War of 1812.

CHAPTER 2

The Story Behind the Glory

How did the United States get its anthem? It is an interesting story—and it begins during the War of 1812. The United States and Great Britain were at war. The United States had declared war after the British began taking U.S. trading ships and blocking U.S. harbors. The British were also forcing U.S. soldiers to fight in their navy.

British troops ate an elegant dinner in the White House before they burned it down.

The British and the Americans fought many battles during the War of 1812, including this attack on Washington, D.C., in 1814.

President James Madison escaped to Virginia before Washington burned.

British forces captured Washington, D.C., on August 24, 1814. They set fire to many buildings, lighting up the night sky. Happy British soldiers headed back to their warships after their victory. Two British soldiers wandered through the nearby city of Baltimore, Maryland. An American doctor named William Beanes tried to have them arrested.

Baltimore, Maryland, is a port city not far from Washington, D.C. This engraving is from the early 1800s.

One of the soldiers escaped and ran to alert more soldiers. British soldiers came and freed their man. Then they arrested the 65-year-old Dr. Beanes instead.

Next, the Americans chose two men to try to free the well-liked Dr. Beanes. One was Francis Scott Key, a 35-year-old lawyer from Maryland who liked to write poetry. The other was a U.S. soldier named John Skinner.

Francis Scott Key

Baltimore Harbor was full of British warships such as this one when Key and Skinner went to free Dr. Beanes.

On a British Warship

Beanes was being held in the middle of Chesapeake Bay on a British warship called the HMS *Tonnant*. Key and Skinner took a small boat out to the British ship. The ship's **admiral**, Alexander Cochrane, gave them permission to board and invited them to dine in his cabin.

After dinner was served, Admiral Cochrane listened as Key shared his thoughts about Dr. Beanes. Key explained that Beanes was not an active soldier but a doctor. Key and Skinner also showed Admiral Cochrane and his men letters written by wounded British soldiers whom Beanes had treated. The letters praised the doctor. Admiral Cochrane was moved. He agreed to free Beanes.

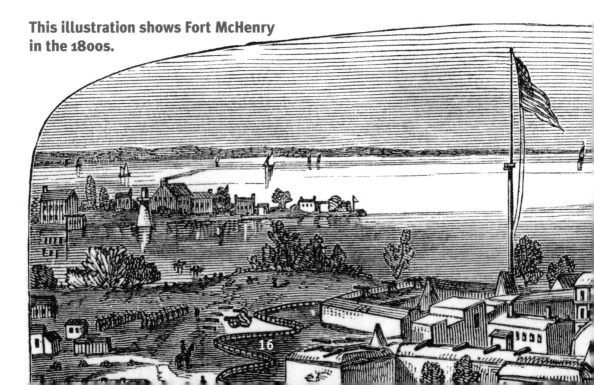

This illustration shows Fort McHenry in the 1800s.

However, the British did not allow Francis Scott Key and John Skinner to return home. Instead, they held the Americans in the small boat the two men had sailed from Baltimore. The boat stayed in the harbor, close to Fort McHenry. The British posted guards to make sure the two men did not escape.

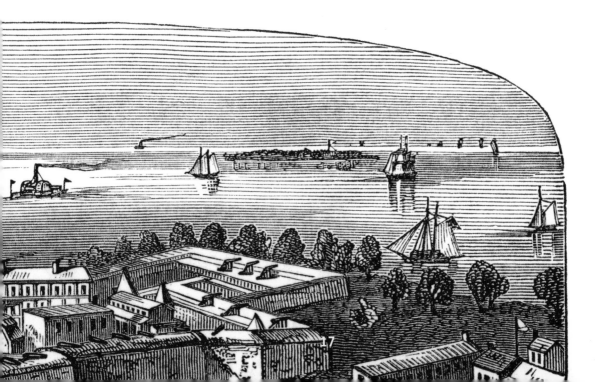

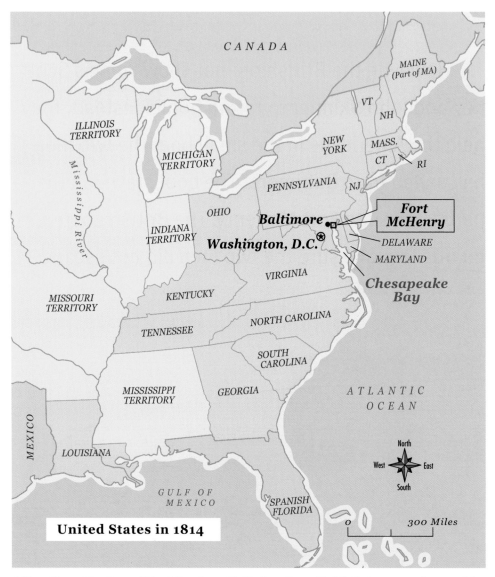

United States in 1814

After the attack on Washington, D.C., in 1814, British troops planned to move north to Baltimore.

A Plan of Attack

The reason for holding the Americans was simple. British forces were planning an attack on the fort guarding Baltimore Harbor, called Fort McHenry. Key and Skinner may have overheard the British plans during their dinner on the ship. The British did not want the men to warn U.S. soldiers.

The British didn't know it, but the U.S. troops at Fort McHenry were already expecting an attack. The Americans realized that Baltimore was the next likely target for the British. And to reach the city of Baltimore, the British had to get past Fort McHenry.

This illustration of Fort McHenry and Chesapeake Bay is from 1862.

Fort McHenry is now a national monument and historic shrine. Exhibits help visitors visualize life at the fort during different stages in its history.

CHAPTER 3

A Special Flag

By presidential order, an American flag must fly over Fort McHenry 24 hours a day.

Major George Armistead became the U.S. commander of Fort McHenry in 1813. He always welcomed challenges and was eager to take on the British. Weeks before the attack on Washington, D.C., Armistead came up with a daring idea. He decided to call attention to the fort by flying a huge flag over it. And he wanted the flag to be special.

"It is my desire," Major Armistead said, "to have a flag so large that the British will have no difficulty seeing it from a distance." It was his way of standing up to the British and showing his confidence in the United States. He ordered this special flag to be made right away.

In Baltimore stands a statue of George Armistead. He commanded the land forces at Fort McHenry during the War of 1812.

A Large Task

Major Armistead hired a Baltimore **widow** named Mary Young Pickersgill for the job. She would actually sew two flags for Fort McHenry, the huge one and a smaller flag for stormy weather.

Pickersgill was a good choice for the job. She ran a successful business making flags. Pickersgill was a "maker of ships' colors" in the Baltimore city directory of 1816. "Ships' colors" are large flags that fly on ships.

This time Pickersgill was asked to make a flag that measured 30 feet by 42 feet (9 meters by 13 meters) to fly over Fort McHenry. That's about the size of half a tennis court! Each star measured 24 inches (61 centimeters) across. The smaller storm flag would measure 17 feet by 25 feet (5 meters by 7.6 meters).

Making a Flag

Pickersgill had to measure, cut, and sew all the pieces of the flag together. She used wool fabric for the stripes and white cotton for the stars. The flag was too big to assemble in her house. Pickersgill and her helpers had to put it together on the floor of a local factory, after work hours.

Mary Young Pickersgill

Women who repaired Pickersgill's flag in 1914 probably made about 1.7 million stitches.

Amelia Fowler and a team of 10 women restore the original Star-Spangled Banner. The work took eight weeks. Fowler charged the Smithsonian Institution $1243: $243 for materials, $500 for herself, and $500 to be divided among the 10 needlewomen.

What Did the Star-Spangled Banner Look Like?

The flag known as the original Star-Spangled Banner looked different from today's flag. The first American flags had a star and a stripe for each of the 13 U.S. states. The Star-Spangled Banner that flew over Fort McHenry had 15 stars and 15 red and white stripes. In fact, there were 18 U.S. states by 1814, but the flag had not yet been

officially changed. The American flag that we use today has 50 stars, one for each state.

Other women, including Pickersgill's 13-year-old daughter, Caroline, helped with the work. Often the women worked by lamplight late into the night. It took six weeks to complete the job! Mary Young Pickersgill was paid $405.90 for the finished flag. Today, that would be close to $5,000.

Pickersgill received this receipt for sewing the Star-Spangled Banner. It is dated October 27, 1813.

The last time he saw it, the flag was waving majestically over the fort. He caught glimpses of it through the darkness as bombs and rockets exploded.

O'er the **ramparts** we watch'd, were so gallantly streaming?

And the rocket's red glare, the bombs bursting in air,

Gave proof through the night that our flag was still there.

O say does that star-spangled banner yet wave

O'er the land of the free and the home of the brave?

Key marveled that the flag survived! Today, flags continue to wave over the land of the free and the home of the brave!

"The Star-Spangled Banner"

You sing it, but have you actually stopped to think about what those lyrics mean?

After a long night of fighting, Key awoke early in the morning and guess what he saw?

O say can you see, by the dawn's early light,

What so proudly we hail'd at the twilight's last gleaming?

Whose broad stripes and bright stars through the perilous fight

He saw the U.S. flag! The night before, he'd saluted it before going to bed.

29

CHAPTER 4

"The Bombs Bursting in Air"

The British hit Fort McHenry with more than 1,500 explosive shells.

The British ships attacked Fort McHenry at dawn on September 13, 1814. There was nothing that Francis Scott Key could do except watch from his small boat. The British ships' **cannons** blasted away for hours. The **shells** pounded throughout the day. Smoke from the exploding shells hung in the air. Soon it became hard for Key to see.

British ships fire cannons on Fort McHenry during the night of September 13–14, 1814.

Things only got worse for the Americans after nightfall. British land troops attacked the fort under the cover of darkness. The ships' cannons continued firing. The rockets' red glare streaked across the night sky. Key feared for the fort.

Hoping to Win

Key was uncertain whether or not Fort McHenry could survive the attack. He feared that the British troops would take over the fort and move on to destroy Baltimore. He could only hope for an American victory.

By the morning of September 14, about 25 hours after the fighting had begun, the smoke cleared. There in the early light, Key could not believe his eyes. He saw the American flag still waving in the breeze! Key knew at that moment that the Americans had won the battle.

In this painting, Francis Scott Key points to the American flag flying above Fort McHenry. John Skinner sits next to Key on the boat.

O say can you see ~~through~~ by the dawn's early light,
What so proudly we hail'd at the twilight's last gleaming,
Whose broad stripes & bright stars through the perilous fight
O'er the ramparts we watch'd, were so gallantly streaming?
And the rocket's red glare, the bomb bursting in air,
Gave proof through the night that our flag was still there,
O say does that star spangled banner yet wave
O'er the land of the free & the home of the brave?

On the shore dimly seen through the mists of the deep,
Where the foe's haughty host in dread silence reposes,
What is that which the breeze, o'er the towering steep,
As it fitfully blows, half conceals, half discloses?
Now it catches the gleam of the morning's first beam,
In full glory reflected now shines in the stream,
'Tis the star-spangled banner — O long may it wave
O'er the land of the free & the home of the brave!

And where is that band who so vauntingly swore,
That the havoc of war & the battle's confusion
A home & a Country should leave us no more?
~~~~
Their blood has wash'd out their foul footstep's pollution.
No refuge could save the hireling & slave
From the terror of flight or the gloom of the grave,
And the star-spangled banner in triumph doth wave
O'er the land of the free & the home of the brave.

O thus be it ever when freemen shall stand
Between their lov'd home & the war's desolation!
Blest with vict'ry & peace may the heav'n rescued land
Praise the power that hath made & preserv'd us a nation!
Then conquer we must, when our cause it is just,
And this be our motto — "In God is our trust,"
And the star-spangled banner in triumph shall wave
O'er the land of the free & the home of the brave. —

Francis Scott Key handwrote this original copy of "The Star-Spangled Banner," a poem, in 1814. It is now on display at the Maryland Historical Society in Baltimore.

Francis Scott Key wrote his poem on the back of a letter.

The flying Star-Spangled Banner inspired Key. He began writing a poem about the battle while he was on the boat. After the battle ended, the British released the two Americans. Key finished his poem the next day. He called it "Defence of Fort M'Henry."

Becoming an Anthem

Francis Scott Key gave the finished poem to his wife's relative, who had **handbills** of it printed. Soon the poem appeared in newspapers in many different cities. Key felt that his poem could also be sung. He chose the tune of an old English song.

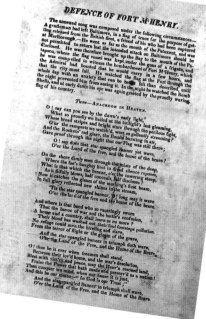

This handbill of Key's poem was printed in 1814. It is one of only two known to exist today.

"The Star-Spangled Banner" Timeline

1794

Congress approves a U.S. flag with 15 stars and 15 stripes. Use of the new flag design begins in 1795.

1814

After the British attack on Fort McHenry, Francis Scott Key completes a poem called "Defence of Fort M'Henry."

Key's poem was sung publicly for the first time on October 19, 1814, at a Baltimore theater. Before long, it was being sung everywhere.

The song later became known as "The Star-Spangled Banner." The banner is the flag Key saw flying over Fort McHenry. It was a sight he would never forget.

1889
"The Star-Spangled Banner" becomes an official U.S. Navy song.

1931
President Herbert Hoover makes "The Star-Spangled Banner" the country's national anthem.

CHAPTER 5

Our National Anthem

More than 70 percent of Americans learned the national anthem in a school music class.

"The Star-Spangled Banner" grew even more popular as time passed. It made everyone proud of the brave soldiers who had fought at Fort McHenry. The men and women of the armed forces especially liked the song. In the 1890s, "The Star-Spangled Banner" became the song used by both the U.S. Navy and Army in official ceremonies.

Later, in 1931, Congress made "The Star-Spangled Banner" our country's national anthem. President Herbert Hoover signed the bill into law on March 3, 1931. Today, people across America regularly sing the song at sporting and other events.

At the Olympic Games, the gold medal winner's national anthem is always played at the medal ceremony.

That Special Flag

So what happened to the flag that flew over Fort McHenry? A few weeks after the battle, Major Armistead gave a soldier's widow a small piece of the flag. She wanted to bury it with her husband.

In later years, people cut off other small pieces. The flag that exists today is about 8 feet (2.4 meters) shorter than it was when it flew over Fort McHenry. Today, that very flag has an honored place in America. It is on display in the National Museum of American History in Washington, D.C.

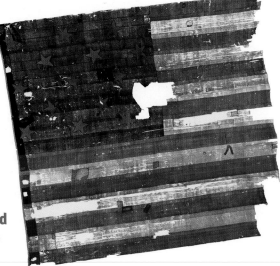

George Armistead's grandson donated the original Star-Spangled Banner to the Smithsonian Institution in 1912.

Experts examine the cloth of the original Star-Spangled Banner. This is part of the process of preserving the flag.

That flag and the poem that Francis Scott Key wrote about it are important national **symbols**. They can make Americans feel proud. They also remind us of how lucky we are. As Francis Scott Key put it, we live in "the land of the free and the home of the brave." ★

Anthem words written by: Francis Scott Key

Original title of poem: "Defence of Fort M'Henry"

Written in: 1814

Number of verses in original poem: Four

Music that the words are sung to: An 18th-century tune by British composer John Stafford Smith

Original draft of poem on display at: Maryland Historical Society in Baltimore, Maryland

Original Star-Spangled Banner sewed in: Baltimore, Maryland, in July–August 1813

Design of Star-Spangled Banner: 15 stars and 15 stripes

DEFENCE OF FORT M'HENRY.

The annexed song was composed under the following circumstances—A gentleman had left Baltimore, in a flag of truce for the purpose of getting released from the British fleet, a friend of his who had been captured at Marlborough.—He went as far as the mouth of the Patuxent, and was not permitted to return lest the intended attack on Baltimore should be disclosed. He was therefore brought up the Bay to the mouth of the Patapsco, where the flag vessel was kept under the guns of a frigate, and he was compelled to witness the bombardment of Fort M'Henry, which the Admiral had boasted that he would carry in a few hours, and that the city must fall. He watched the flag at the Fort thr whole day with an anxiety that can be better felt than descr the night prevented him from seeing it. In the night he watched Shells, and at early dawn his eye was again greeted by the prou flag of his country.

Tune—ANACREON IN HEAVEN.

O ! say can you see by the dawn's early light,
What so proudly we hailed at the twilight's last gleaming,
Whose broad stripes and bright stars through the perilous fight
O'er the ramparts we watch'd, were so gallantly stream
And the Rockets' red glare, the Bombs bursting in air,
Gave proof through the night that our Flag was still the

O ! say does that star-spangled Banner yet wave
O'er the Land of the free, and the home of the b

On the shore dimly seen through the mists of the deep,
Where the foe's haughty host in dread silence reposes,
What is that which the breeze, o'er the towering steep,
As it fitfully blows, half conceals, half discloses ?
Now it catches the gleam of the morning's first beam,
In full glory reflected new shines in the stream,
'Tis the star spangled banner, O ! long may it wave
O'er the lar d of the free and the home of the brave.

that band who so vauntingly swore
's confusion.

Did you find the truth?

T "The Star-Spangled Banner" was written the morning after a battle.

F The writer of "The Star-Spangled Banner" wrote the words to another national anthem.

Resources

Books

Bowdish, Lynea. *Francis Scott Key and "The Star-Spangled Banner."* New York: Mondo, 2002.

Gray, Susan Heinrichs. *The American Flag.* Minneapolis: Compass Point Books, 2002.

Gregson, Susan R. *Francis Scott Key.* Mankato, MN: Bridgestone Books, 2003.

Hess, Debra. *The Star-Spangled Banner.* New York: Benchmark Books, 2004.

Ingram, Scott. *The Writing of "The Star-Spangled Banner."* Milwaukee: World Almanac Library, 2004.

Landau, Elaine. *The American Flag.* Danbury, CT: Children's Press, 2008.

Pearl, Norman. *Our National Anthem.* Minneapolis: Picture Window Books, 2006.

Webster, Christine. *The Pledge of Allegiance.* Danbury, CT: Children's Press, 2003.

Welch, Catherine A. *The Star-Spangled Banner.* Minneapolis: Carolrhoda Books, 2005.

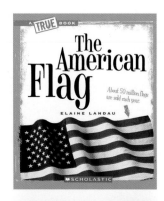

Organizations and Web Sites

National Anthem Project

www.nationalanthemproject.org/

Check out this Web site to learn about the campaign to support music in schools.

Star-Spangled Banner

http://americanhistory.si.edu/ssb/2_home/fs2.html

Visit the Smithsonian Institute's online exhibit.

Places to Visit

Flag House and Star-Spangled Banner Museum

844 East Pratt Street
Baltimore, MD 21202
410-837-1793
www.flaghouse.org/

Visit the museum dedicated to Mary Young Pickersgill, who sewed the enormous flag that flew over Fort McHenry.

Fort McHenry National Monument

2400 East Fort Avenue
Baltimore, MD 21230
410-962-4290
www.nps.gov/fomc/

See the fort that flew the original Star-Spangled Banner.

Maryland Historical Society

201 West Monument Street
Baltimore, MD 21201
410-685-3750
www.mdhs.org/

See the draft of Francis Scott Key's poem.

Important Words

admiral – an officer who ranks above a vice admiral in the navy or coast guard

banner – a specially designed piece of fabric that a nation or organization uses as a symbol or decoration

cannons – large heavy guns that fire a type of shell called a cannonball

handbills – small printed sheets made to be handed out

national anthem (NA-shuh-nl AN-thuhm) – an official song that shows people's pride in their country

patriotic (PAY-tree-AW-tik) – showing pride in and love for one's country

ramparts – the walls that surround a fort to protect against attacks

shells – small bombs fired from a cannon or other weapon

symbols (SIM-bulz) – objects that represent something else such as an idea or a feeling

widow – a woman whose husband has died

Index

About the Author

Award-winning author Elaine Landau has written more than 300 books for children and young adults. She worked as a newspaper reporter, a children's book editor, and a youth services librarian before becoming a full-time writer.

Ms. Landau lives in Miami, Florida, with her husband and their son, Michael. She enjoys writing about history and often visits the places she writes about. You can visit her at her Web site: www.elainelandau.com.